Midjourney Prompts Book

Up to 300 Cliparts & Illustrations

Christmas Edition

Dima Keyi

Midjourney Prompts Book. Up to 300 Cliparts & Illustrations. Christmas Edition
by Dima Keyi

ISBN: 9798866435128

Cover design and book layout by Dima Keyi
Illustrations by Midjourney

First Edition

https://movetoai.tech/

hello@movetoai.tech

Table of Content

Intro 4

Animals in the Holiday Spirit 11

Christmas Objects Come to Life 18

Festive Feasts for the Eyes 28

Christmas Characters Galore 33

Action-Packed Holiday Scenes 38

Inside a Christmas Haven 45

Yuletide in the City 49

Nature's Winter Cloak 54

Outdoor Festivities Unfold 58

Ornamental Stories 62

Contacts 65

Intro

Welcome! You're about to tap into the festive spirit like never before. This book is your toolkit for uncovering the magic of Christmas through digital art using the Midjourney.

Inside, you'll find up to 300 prompts to spark your creativity and celebrate the season in style. Whether you're looking to craft a winter wonderland, a cozy fireside scene, or the joy of Santa's workshop, these prompts are your starting point for creation.

So please grab a cup of hot cocoa, settle in, and let's start crafting your holiday masterpieces.

Step 1: Getting Set Up with Discord

First things first, let's get you set up on Discord, the home base for the Midjourney tool. If you're new to it, think of Discord as a supercharged chat room, perfect for collaboration and community. Head over to https://discord.com/ to sign up. You can use your web browser or download the app for a more robust experience.

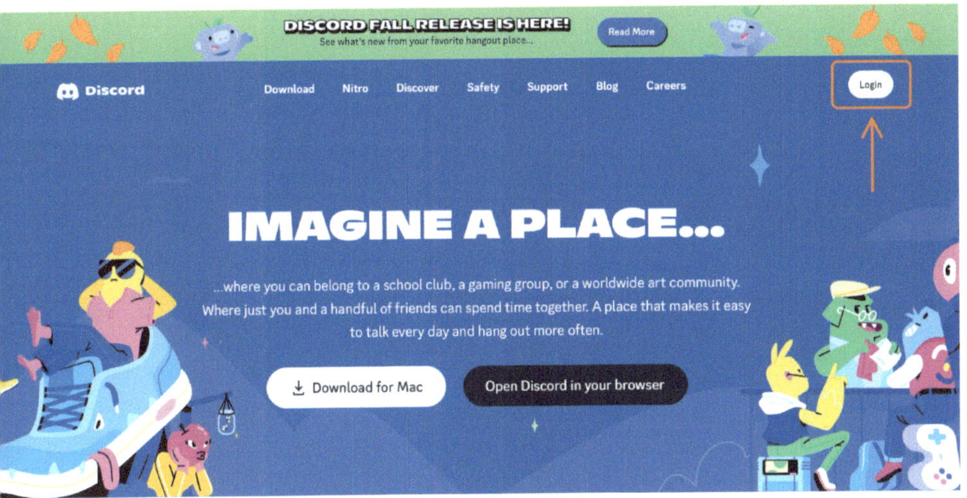

PIC. 1 — SCREENSHOT: DISCORD'S WELCOME PAGE

Step 2: Joining the Midjourney Server

Got your Discord ready? Great! Now, click on https://midjourney.com/ and hit "Join the Beta." Sign in with your Discord details, and just like that, you're in the Midjourney server, where creativity is the name of the game.

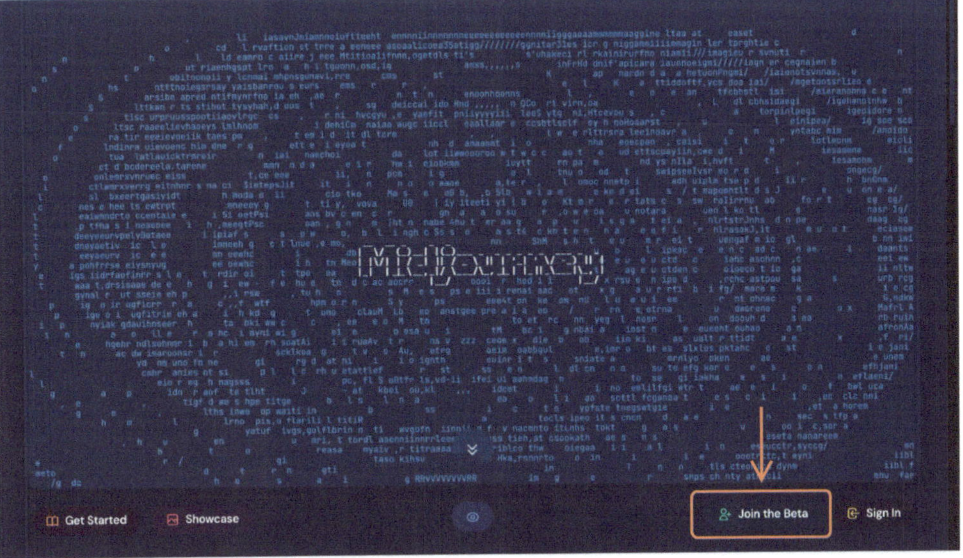

PIC. 2 — SCREENSHOT: MIDJOURNEY'S LANDING PAGE

Step 3: Finding Your Creative Space

Inside the Midjourney server, look for the "**#Newbies**" or "**#General**" channels.
This is where you'll set up shop and start the art-making magic.

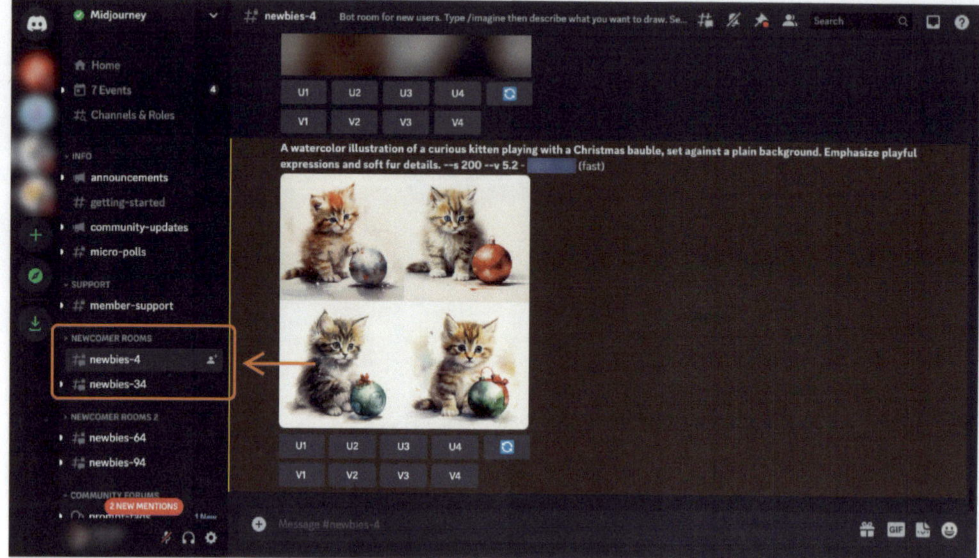

PIC. 4 — SCREENSHOT: MIDJOURNEY'S CHANNELS

Step 4: Chatting with the AI – The /imagine Command

Jump into a channel and get ready to meet Midjourney's AI, your new silent partner in art.

PIC. 5 — SCREENSHOT: AN EMPTY COMMAND LINE

Type '/imagine' into the chat, and a prompt box will pop up, ready for your command.

PIC. 6 — SCREENSHOT: THE COMMAND LINE WITH '/IMAGINE' COMMAND

Here's where you'll type in your artistic prompt, a short description that captures what you want to create.

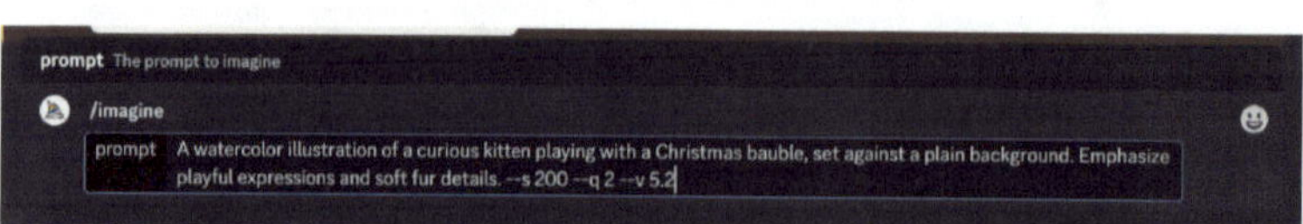

PIC. 7 — SCREENSHOT: YOUR ARTISTIC PROMPT

Don't worry, you'll find plenty of prompt examples as you flip through this book.

tep 5: Playing by the Rules – Terms of Service

efore you bring your ideas to life, you'll need to nod to the Terms of Service. It's all about eeping the creative space positive and respectful.

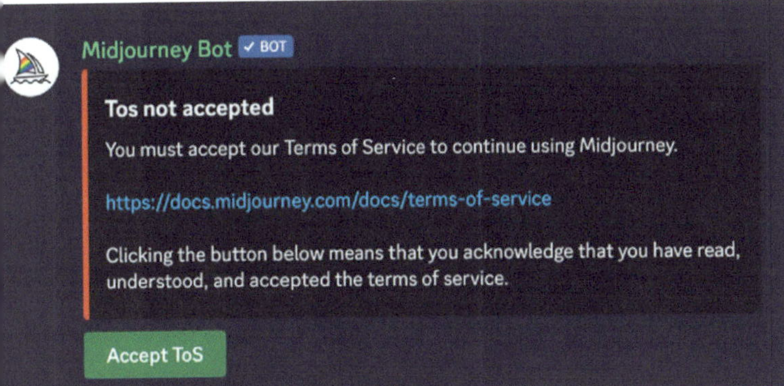

IC. 8 — SCREENSHOT: MIDJOURNEY'S TERMS OF SERVICE

Step 6: Creating Your Art

Once you've agreed to the terms, it's showtime. Enter your prompt and watch the Midjourney bot whip up four different takes on your idea. This is where your art starts to ake shape.

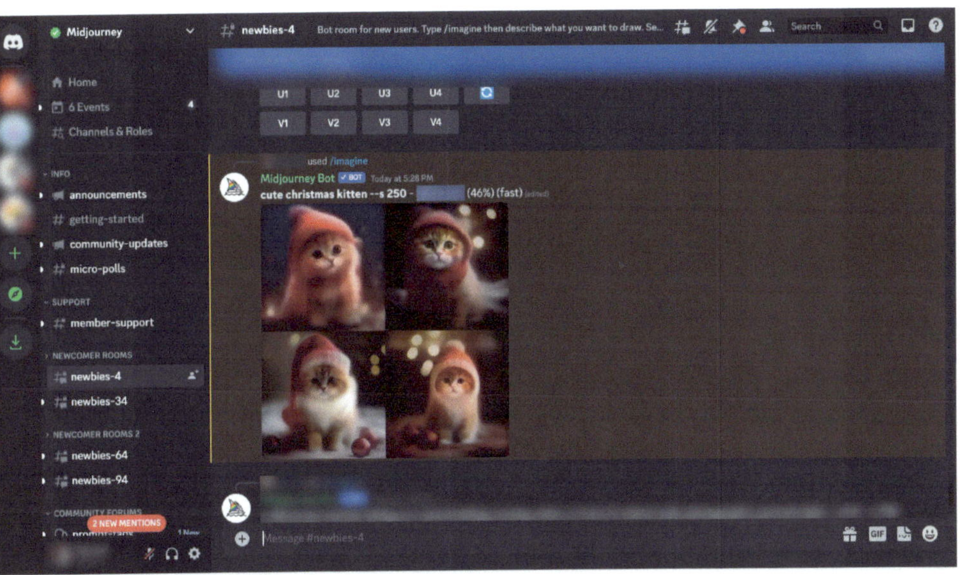

PIC. 9 — SCREENSHOT: THE CREATION PROCESS

Step 7: Fine-Tuning Your Masterpiece

Take a look at what the bot's cooked up. Want to tweak an image? Hit the 'U' button to upscale or 'V' to see variations. Choose the number that corresponds to the image you want to work with.

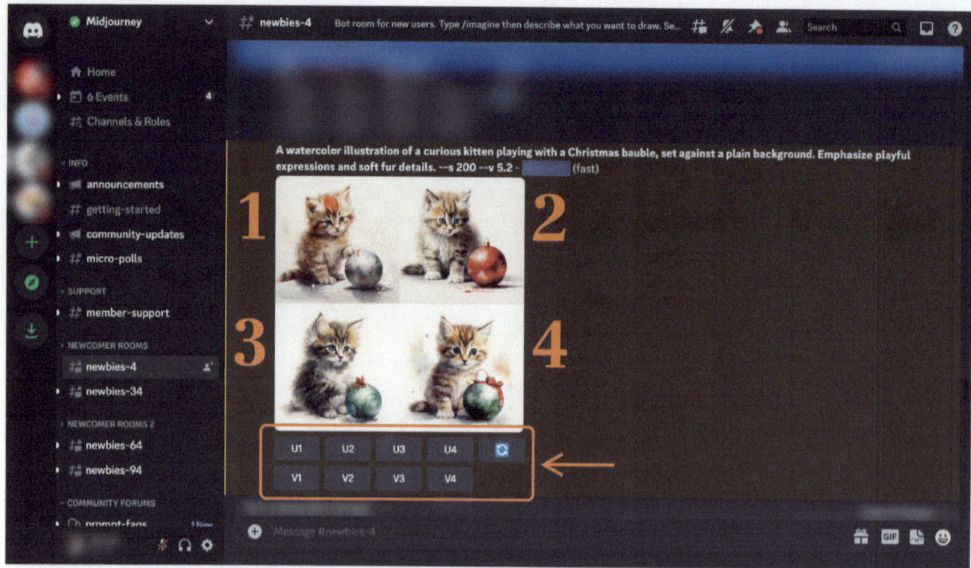

PIC. 10 — SCREENSHOT: IMAGE OPTIONS

Step 8: Expanding Your View

Need to see more of your picture? Use the zoom and pan options to get a wider angle on your artwork.

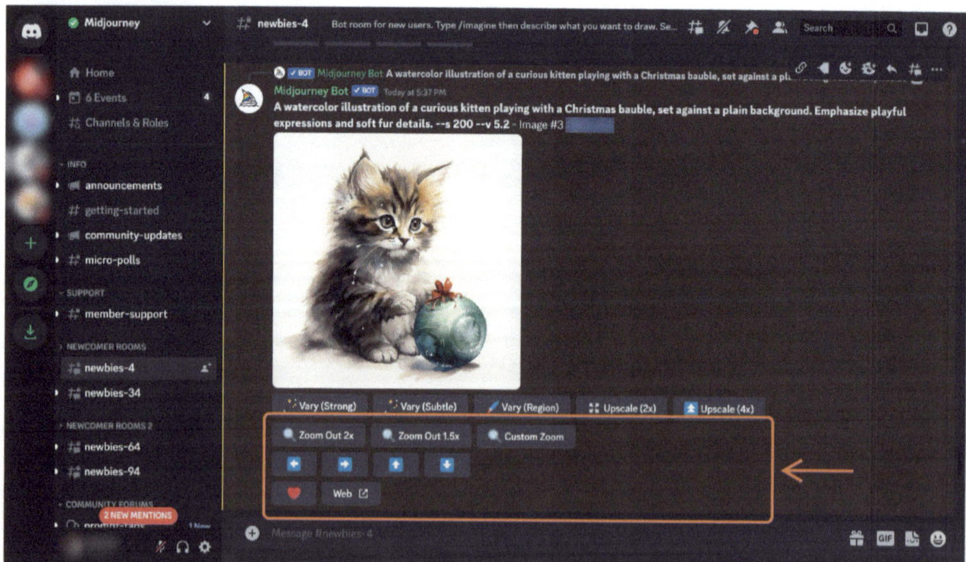

PIC. 11 — SCREENSHOT: ZOOM AND PAN FEATURES

Step 9: Saving Your Work

When you've got that perfect image, save it. Just click, right-click, and choose "Save Image as..." to keep it forever.

PIC. 12 — SCREENSHOT: YOUR FINISHED ARTWORK

Outro: Making the Most of This Book

The following pages are filled with Christmas-themed prompts, each with its own ID, title, and example image. When you're ready to create, just copy a prompt into the '/imagine' command and let the magic happen.

Animals

ID	NAME	PROMPT	SAMPLE RESULT
AN08	Deer v.2	A majestic watercolor painting of a deer with antlers adorned with festive ornaments. The backdrop is a snowy meadow under the Christmas moonlight. --s 200 --q 2 --v 5.2	
AN09	Kitten v.1	A watercolor illustration of a curious kitten playing with a Christmas bauble, set against a plain background. Emphasize playful expressions and soft fur details. --s 200 --q 2 --v 5.2	
AN10	Kitten v.2	A sleeping kitten wrapped in a festive blanket, painted in watercolor. Set within a cozy Christmas environment.	

PIC. 13 — SCREENSHOT: THE BOOK'S LAYOUT

With these steps, you're all set to explore Midjourney's digital canvas. Each prompt you use peels back another layer of your creativity, adding your unique touch to the world of digital art. What will your next creation be? I can't wait to see.

Happy creating!

A Few More Tips Before You Go

For Realistic Creations

Add '--v 5.2' to your prompt to use the latest Midjourney bot version for ultra-realistic images. Or play around with '--v 4' or '--v 3' for a different artistic feel.

Aspect Ratio Adjustments

Your canvas starts as a square, but don't let that box you in. Change it up with '--ar 4:5' for Instagram-ready art or '--ar 16:9' for a widescreen effect.

Style Variations

Dial up the style with '--s'. Start with the guide's '--s 200' and experiment up to '--s 1000' to find the perfect expression for your art.

Check out how the same prompt changes with different '--s' values:

A watercolor illustration of a curious kitten playing with a Christmas bauble, set against a plain background. Emphasize playful expressions and soft fur details.
--s [number] --q 2 --v 5.2

--S 200

--S 500

--S 1000

Now, let's get started!

Animals in the Holiday Spirit

Imagine a winter wonderland where animals join in the holiday cheer. Picture reindeer frolicking in the fresh snow, cozy cats napping near the crackling fire, and cheerful birds decorating the frosty branches.

Animals

ID	NAME	PROMPT	SAMPLE RESULT
AN01	Fox v.1	A watercolor painting of a fox wearing a festive red scarf, surrounded by snow. The mood is serene with a plain background. Emphasize soft brushwork. --s 200 --q 2 --v 5.2	
AN02	Fox v.2	A watercolor depiction of a playful fox with Christmas lights tangled around its tail against a snowy backdrop. Gentle shading and a joyful tone. --s 200 --q 2 --v 5.2	
AN03	Owl v.1	A watercolor portrait of an owl perched on a mistletoe branch, wearing a Santa hat. White background with detailed feathers. --s 200 --q 2 --v 5.2	
AN04	Owl v.2	An owl in flight carrying a festive message in its beak, painted in watercolor. Capture the silent beauty of a snowy night. Plain background. --s 200 --q 2 --v 5.2	
AN05	Forest Animals v.1	A serene watercolor depiction of forest animals exchanging Christmas gifts against white background. Set at dusk with a golden hue, emphasizing the spirit of giving. --s 200 --q 2 --v 5.2	
AN06	Forest Animals v.2	Watercolor scene of a gathering of forest animals around a Christmas tree in the woods. The scene is heartwarming, focusing on unity. Rich and deep colors. --s 200 --q 2 --v 5.2	
AN07	Deer v.1	Watercolor of a fawn with a bright red nose, standing shyly against a snowy white isolated background. Capture innocence and wonder. --s 200 --q 2 --v 5.2	

Animals

ID	NAME	PROMPT	SAMPLE RESULT
AN08	Deer v.2	A majestic watercolor painting of a deer with antlers adorned with festive ornaments. The backdrop is a snowy meadow under the Christmas moonlight. --s 200 --q 2 --v 5.2	
AN09	Kitten v.1	A watercolor illustration of a curious kitten playing with a Christmas bauble, set against a plain background. Emphasize playful expressions and soft fur details. --s 200 --q 2 --v 5.2	
AN10	Kitten v.2	A sleeping kitten wrapped in a festive blanket, painted in watercolor. Set within a cozy Christmas environment with a warm and gentle mood. --s 200 --q 2 --v 5.2	
AN11	Horse v.1	A horse adorned with bells and festive attire, standing against a snowy backdrop. Use watercolor to emphasize the elegance and grace of the animal. --s 200 --q 2 --v 5.2	
AN12	Horse v.2	A watercolor portrayal of a horse pulling a festive sleigh through a snow-covered village. The scene is vibrant, capturing the joy of the season. --s 200 --q 2 --v 5.2	
AN13	Dog v.1	A cheerful watercolor painting of a dog wearing christmast reindeer antlers, set against a white background. Focus on the dog's joyful expression. --s 200 --q 2 --v 5.2	
AN14	Dog v.2	A watercolor scene of a dog excitedly unwrapping a Christmas gift. Emphasize the festive chaos and playful energy. --s 200 --q 2 --v 5.2	

Animals

ID	NAME	PROMPT	SAMPLE RESULT
AN15	Squirrel v.1	Watercolor depiction of a squirrel holding a shiny Christmas bauble, with a snowy forest isolated white backdrop. Capture the creature's mischievous nature. --s 200 --q 2 --v 5.2	
AN16	Squirrel v.2	A squirrel with a Santa hat, nibbling on a pinecone. Use watercolors to set the scene in a snow-covered park. --s 200 --q 2 --v 5.2	
AN17	Mice (Mouse) v.1	A watercolor painting of a mouse wearing a festive sweater, set against a plain background. Emphasize delicate brushwork and a serene mood. --s 200 --q 2 --v 5.2	
AN18	Mice (Mouse) v.2	Watercolor scene of mice preparing a Christmas feast, capturing the hustle and bustle of the festive preparations. --s 200 --q 2 --v 5.2	
AN19	Polar bear v.1	Polar bear wearing a festive Christmas scarf, with snowflakes gently falling around, isolated white background. Use watercolor to capture the serene beauty of the Arctic. --s 200 --q 2 --v 5.2	
AN20	Polar bear v.2	A watercolor of a polar bear with cubs, amidst a snowy landscape. Set the scene under the Northern Lights, capturing wonder and awe. --s 200 --q 2 --v 5.2	
AN21	Swan v.1	Swans with festive crowns, gracefully gliding on water, isolated white background. Use watercolors to capture the reflection and tranquility of the Christmas scene. --s 200 --q 2 --v 5.2	

Animals

ID	NAME	PROMPT	SAMPLE RESULT
AN22	Swan v.2	A watercolor portrayal of a swan swimming in a frozen lake, surrounded by soft snowfall. Emphasize the elegance and serenity of the moment. --s 200 --q 2 --v 5.2	
AN23	Winter Robin v.1	Watercolor illustration of a winter robin perched on a festive wreath, set against a plain background. Emphasize the bird's vibrant colors. --s 200 --q 2 --v 5.2	
AN24	Winter Robin v.2	A cheerful robin with a sprig of holly, painted in watercolor against a snowy backdrop. Capture the essence of winter's beauty. --s 200 --q 2 --v 5.2	
AN25	Penguin v.1	Penguin wearing a Santa hat, sliding down an icy slope on isolated white background. Use watercolors to bring out the fun and playfulness of the scene. --s 200 --q 2 --v 5.2	
AN26	Penguin v.2	A watercolor scene of penguins exchanging gifts against an Antarctic sunset. The mood is jovial, capturing the spirit of giving. --s 200 --q 2 --v 5.2	
AN27	Hedgehog v.1	Watercolor painting of a hedgehog with a festive bow, set against a white background. Emphasize soft spines and a gentle demeanor. --s 200 --q 2 --v 5.2	
AN28	Hedgehog v.2	A hedgehog nestled amidst Christmas ornaments. Paint in watercolor to emphasize the contrast of textures and festive surroundings. --s 200 --q 2 --v 5.2	

Animals

ID	NAME	PROMPT	SAMPLE RESULT
AN29	Christmas ducks v.1	Watercolor depiction of ducks with festive Christmas hats, wading in a frozen pond, isolated white background. Capture the reflection and serenity of a winter's day. --s 200 --q 2 --v 5.2	
AN30	Christmas ducks v.2	Ducks carrying festive gifts in a snowy environment. Use watercolors to showcase the vibrant colors against the snowy backdrop. --s 200 --q 2 --v 5.2	
AN31	Festive rabbits v.1	A watercolor painting of Christmas rabbits wearing festive sweaters, surrounded by snow-covered carrots on isolated white background. Capture the warmth and joy of the scene. --s 200 --q 2 --v 5.2	
AN32	Festive rabbits v.2	Rabbits exchanging Christmas gifts under a moonlit sky. Emphasize the soft fur and gentle mood using watercolors. --s 200 --q 2 --v 5.2	
AN33	Snowy goose v.1	A goose adorned with festive garlands, set against a snowy backdrop. Capture the elegance and grace using watercolors. --s 200 --q 2 --v 5.2	
AN34	Snowy goose v.2	Watercolor scene of a goose in a snow-covered field, with Christmas motif. Emphasize the contrast of the goose's feathers against the pristine snow. Plain background. --s 200 --q 2 --v 5.2	
AN35	Christmas butterfly v.1	Watercolor depiction of a butterfly with festive patterns, resting on a Christmas ornament. Emphasize vibrant colors and delicate wings. --s 200 --q 2 --v 5.2	

Animals

ID	NAME	PROMPT	SAMPLE RESULT
AN36	Christmas butterfly v.2	Butterfly amidst a snowy landscape, its wings resembling festive decorations. Use watercolor to capture its beauty against the white snow. --s 200 --q 2 --v 5.2	
AN37	Reindeer v.1	Watercolor reindeer with Christmas festive bells on the neck, in a snow-covered forest, isolated white background. Use watercolors to capture the lively mood and snowy environment. --s 200 --q 2 --v 5.2	
AN38	Reindeer v.2	A watercolor painting of a reindeer with a glowing nose, set against the Northern Lights. Emphasize the magical and enchanting atmosphere. --s 200 --q 2 --v 5.2	

Christmas Objects Come to Life

Envision the quintessential Christmas scene with gifts wrapped in shiny paper under the tree, old-fashioned sleighs ready for a ride, and baubles that carry stories of yesteryears.

Objects

ID	NAME	PROMPT	SAMPLE RESULT
OBJ01	Crystal Snow Ball v.1	Watercolor illustration of a crystal snow ball, inside a snowy village scene with children playing. Isolated white background. Detailed brushwork for the snowflakes inside. Format: miniature. --s 200 --q 2 --v 5.2	
OBJ02	Crystal Snow Ball v.2	Watercolor scene of a crystal snow ball, capturing a serene winter landscape with a lone cabin. Light background. Emphasize reflections on the globe's surface. Format: wintry wonder. --s 200 --q 2 --v 5.2	
OBJ03	Festive Train v.1	Watercolor portrayal of a festive train with presents piled up in the carts, smoke rising from the engine shaped like candy canes. Isolated white background. Format: holiday express. --s 200 -- q 2 --v 5.2	
OBJ04	Festive Train v.2	Watercolor illustration of a vintage festive train, adorned with lights and holly, passing through a snowy landscape. Plain background. Detailing on the train's ornate carriages. --s 200 --q 2 --v 5.2	
OBJ05	Christmas Wreath v.1	Watercolor depiction of a lush Christmas wreath, adorned with red berries, pine cones, and golden ribbons. Isolated white background. Layered brushwork for depth. Format: doorway delight. --s 200 --q 2 --v 5.2	
OBJ06	Christmas Wreath v.2	Watercolor scene of a rustic Christmas wreath, crafted from twigs and adorned with dried orange slices and cinnamon sticks. Light background. Emphasize the natural elements. Format: charm. --s 200 --q 2 --v 5.2	
OBJ07	Teddy Bear v.1	Watercolor illustration of a plush teddy bear, dressed in a Santa hat and scarf, clutching a tiny gift. Isolated white background. Soft brushwork for the fur texture. --s 200 --q 2 --v 5.2	

Objects

ID	NAME	PROMPT	SAMPLE RESULT
OBJ08	Teddy Bear v.2	Watercolor scene of an old-fashioned teddy bear, seated under the tree, awaiting Christmas morning. Plain background. Detailed strokes. Format: vintage nostalgia. --s 200 --q 2 --v 5.2	
OBJ09	Presents v.1	Watercolor portrayal of a pile of wrapped presents, ribbons cascading, tags written with love. Among them, one box stands out with a big, shiny bow. Isolated white background. Format: festive bounty. --s 200 --q 2 --v 5.2	
OBJ10	Presents v.2	Watercolor scene of presents neatly stacked by the fireplace, stockings hung above, awaiting Christmas morning. Light background. Delicate detailing on the intricate wrapping patterns. --s 200 -- q 2 --v 5.2	
OBJ11	Whimsical Ice Skates v.1	Watercolor depiction of whimsical ice skates shoes, their scarves flowing in the winter breeze. Glimmering snowflakes drift around them. Isolated white background. Delicate strokes. --s 200 --q 2 --v 5.2	
OBJ12	Whimsical Ice Skates v.2	Watercolor scene of a pair of whimsical ice skates. Light background. Emphasis on their shadows reflecting on the icy surface. Format: moonlit waltz. --s 200 --q 2 --v 5.2	
OBJ13	Festive Lantern v.1	Watercolor illustration of a festive lantern, glowing warmly with a candle inside, surrounded by holly and berries. Isolated white background. Soft glow emanating from the lantern. --s 200 --q 2 --v 5.2	
OBJ14	Festive Lantern v.2	Watercolor scene of a festive lantern, nestled in snow, its light casting long shadows on the snow-covered ground. Plain background. Focus on the play of light and shadow. Format: winter beacon. --s 200 --q 2 --v 5.2	

Objects

ID	NAME	PROMPT	SAMPLE RESULT
OBJ15	Christmas Baubles v.1	Watercolor portrayal of glistening Christmas baubles, hanging delicately from evergreen branches, reflecting the festive lights. Isolated white background. Use reflective technique. Format: holiday. --s 200 --q 2 --v 5.2	
OBJ16	Christmas Baubles v.2	Watercolor scene of an assortment of Christmas baubles, lying on a wooden table, ready to be hung. Light background. Detailed patterns on the ornaments. Format: festive collection. --s 200 --q 2 --v 5.2	
OBJ17	Christmas Tree v.1	Watercolor depiction of a majestic Christmas tree, adorned with twinkling fairy lights, tinsel, and a shining star on top. Presents piled below. Isolated white background. Format: celebration. --s 200 -- q 2 --v 5.2	
OBJ18	Christmas Tree v.2	Watercolor scene of a rustic Christmas tree, decorated with hand-made ornaments, popcorn garlands, and wooden toys. Plain background. Emphasis on the home-made details. --s 200 --q 2 --v 5.2	
OBJ19	Christmas Star v.1	Watercolor illustration of a radiant Christmas star, shimmering in gold and silver, casting a gentle glow. Isolated white background. Soft gradient for the luminescence. Format: guiding star. --s 200 --q 2 --v 5.2	
OBJ20	Christmas Star v.2	Watercolor scene of a Christmas star, perched atop a tree, with the night sky and moon as a backdrop. Light background. Detailed patterns on the star's ornaments. Format: celestial celebration. --s 200 --q 2 --v 5.2	
OBJ21	Christmas Stocking v.1	Watercolor rendering of a plush Christmas stocking, adorned with festive motifs and filled to the brim with toys and candies. Isolated white background. Stitched detailing for a hand-made look. --s 200 --q 2 --v 5.2	

Objects

ID	NAME	PROMPT	SAMPLE RESULT
OBJ22	Christmas Stocking v.2	Watercolor scene of a row of Christmas stockings, hung by the fireplace, each unique in design and waiting to be filled. Light background. Texture emphasis on the stocking material. --s 200 --q 2 --v 5.2	
OBJ23	Poinsettia Plant v.1	Watercolor portrayal of a vibrant poinsettia plant, its red leaves contrasting with green foliage. Isolated white background. Velvety texture for the leaves. Format: festive flora. --s 200 --q 2 --v 5.2	
OBJ24	Poinsettia Plant v.2	Watercolor scene of a poinsettia plant placed on a windowsill, snow falling gently outside. Plain background. Focus on the snowy ambiance. Format: winter bloom. --s 200 -- q 2 --v 5.2	
OBJ25	Fairy Lights v.1	Watercolor depiction of fairy lights, twinkling in various colors, draped elegantly over a mantelpiece. Isolated white background. Delicate brushwork for the tiny lights. Format: magical luminescence --s 200 --q 2 --v 5.2	
OBJ26	Fairy Lights v.2	Watercolor scene of a garden lit by fairy lights, creating a magical nighttime wonderland. Light background. Emphasis on the ambient glow. Format: enchanted evening. --s 200 --q 2 --v 5.2	
OBJ27	Pine Branch v.1	Watercolor illustration of a snow-kissed pine branch, with pinecones hanging and a backdrop of falling snow. Isolated white background. Detailed brushwork on the pine needles. Format: winter's touch. --s 200 --q 2 --v 5.2	
OBJ28	Pine Branch v.2	Watercolor scene of a pine branch adorned with Christmas baubles and tinsel, ready to be placed on the festive table. Plain background. Emphasis on festive decorations. Format: natural decor. --s 200 --q 2 --v 5.2	

Objects

ID	NAME	PROMPT	SAMPLE RESULT
OBJ29	Candy Cane v.1	Watercolor portrayal of candy canes, with their iconic red and white swirls, nestled amidst holly and berries. Isolated white background. Glossy finish on the candy. Format: sugary delight. --s 200 --q 2 --v 5.2	
OBJ30	Candy Cane v.2	Watercolor scene of candy canes arranged in a heart shape on a rustic wooden table. Light background. Focus on the sweet sentiment. Format: festive love. --s 200 --q 2 --v 5.2	
OBJ31	Christmas Cracker v.1	Watercolor depiction of a festive Christmas cracker, adorned with ribbons and ready to be pulled. Isolated white background. Emphasis on vibrant colors and patterns. Format: festive pop. --s 200 -- q 2 --v 5.2	
OBJ32	Christmas Cracker v.2	Watercolor scene of hands eagerly pulling a Christmas cracker, surprises ready to spring forth. Plain background. Action and anticipation captured in brush strokes. Format: celebration moment --s 200 --q 2 --v 5.2	
OBJ33	Christmas Candle v.1	Watercolor illustration of a Christmas candle, burning bright with a festive wreath around its base. Isolated white background. Warm glow captured with soft gradients. Format: beacon of hope. --s 200 --q 2 --v 5.2	
OBJ34	Christmas Candle v.2	Watercolor scene of a trio of Christmas candles, casting a serene glow on a festive table setting. Light background. Emphasis on the ambiance they create. Format: luminary trio. --s 200 --q 2 --v 5.2	
OBJ35	Nutcracker Soldier v.1	Watercolor portrayal of a majestic nutcracker soldier, standing tall in his vibrant uniform, complete with a tall hat. Isolated white background. Fine detailing on the uniform. Format: holiday guard. --s 200 --q 2 --v 5.2	

Objects

ID	NAME	PROMPT	SAMPLE RESULT
OBJ36	Nutcracker Soldier v.2	Watercolor scene of a nutcracker soldier on a mantelpiece, surrounded by festive ornaments and twinkling fairy lights. Plain background. Format: sentinel of joy. --s 200 --q 2 --v 5.2	
OBJ37	Jingle Bell v.1	Watercolor rendition of a gleaming jingle bell, its metallic surface reflecting festive lights, complete with a red ribbon. Isolated white background. Shimmering effect on the metal. --s 200 --q 2 --v 5.2	
OBJ38	Jingle Bell v.2	Watercolor scene of jingle bells strung together, creating a melodious chime with every gust of winter wind. Light background. Musical ambiance. Format: Christmas chimes. --s 200 -- q 2 --v 5.2	
OBJ39	Gingerbread House v.1	Watercolor illustration of an intricate gingerbread house, adorned with candy canes, colorful icing, and gumdrops. Isolated white background. Fine detailing on the edible decorations. --s 200 --q 2 --v 5.2	
OBJ40	Gingerbread House v.2	Watercolor scene of children joyfully building a gingerbread house, with bowls of sweets and frosting at hand. Plain background. Focus on the playful creativity. Format: festive workshop. --s 200 --q 2 --v 5.2	
OBJ41	Gingerbread Man v.1	Watercolor depiction of a delightful gingerbread man, decorated with icing buttons and a cheerful face. Isolated white background. Texture emphasis for a freshly baked feel. --s 200 --q 2 --v 5.2	
OBJ42	Gingerbread Man v.2	Watercolor scene of gingerbread men and women, creating a festive parade on a snowy landscape. Light background. Emphasis on the merry gathering. Format: sweet march. --s 200 --q 2 --v 5.2	

Objects

ID	NAME	PROMPT	SAMPLE RESULT
OBJ43	Victorian Advent Calendar v.1	Watercolor portrayal of a Victorian-style advent calendar, with ornate windows revealing festive treats and scenes. Isolated white background. Delicate brushwork for the vintage details. --s 200 --q 2 --v 5.2	
OBJ44	Victorian Advent Calendar v.2	Watercolor scene of hands eagerly opening a window of a Victorian advent calendar, anticipation in the air. Plain background. Focus on the surprise element. Format: day of delight. --s 200 --q 2 --v 5.2	
OBJ45	Vintage Christmas Radio v.1	Watercolor illustration of a vintage Christmas radio, broadcasting festive tunes, adorned with a holly sprig. Isolated white background. Emphasis on retro design. Format: yuletide broadcast. --s 200 -- q 2 --v 5.2	
OBJ46	Vintage Christmas Radio v.2	Watercolor scene of a family gathered around a vintage Christmas radio, lost in the melodies of Christmas past. Light background. Emotion captured in their expressions. Format: nostalgic tunes. --s 200 --q 2 --v 5.2	
OBJ47	Snow-covered Pinecone v.1	Watercolor rendering of a pinecone, blanketed in fresh snow, capturing the essence of a white Christmas. Isolated white background. Detailed brushwork on the snowy texture. Format: winter's jewel. --s 200 --q 2 --v 5.2	
OBJ48	Snow-covered Pinecone v.2	Watercolor scene of snow-covered pinecones adorning a festive table, adding a touch of natural beauty. Plain background. Emphasis on the rustic ambiance. Format: nature's ornament. --s 200 --q 2 --v 5.2	
OBJ49	Frosty Snowflakes v.1	Watercolor depiction of intricate snowflakes, each unique and detailed, capturing the magic of winter. Isolated white background. Crystal-like brushwork for realism. Format: frozen fractals. --s 200 --q 2 --v 5.2	

Objects

ID	NAME	PROMPT	SAMPLE RESULT
OBJ50	Mistletoe	Watercolor illustration of a sprig of mistletoe, with its green leaves and white berries, symbolizing festive romance. Isolated white background. Delicate details on the plant's texture. --s 200 --q 2 --v 5.2	
OBJ51	Carol Book v.1	Watercolor rendition of a vintage carol book, opened to display classic Christmas hymns. Isolated white background. Fine detailing on the aged pages and handwritten notes. --s 200 --q 2 --v 5.2	
OBJ52	Carol Book v.2	Watercolor scene of hands holding a carol book, surrounded by a choir in mid-song. Light background. Emphasis on the collective joy of singing. Format: voices in harmony. --s 200 -- q 2 --v 5.2	
OBJ53	Festive Mailbox v.1	Watercolor portrayal of a festive mailbox, adorned with holly and ribbons, awaiting Christmas cards. Isolated white background. Detailing on the rustic metal and decorations. Format: messages of joy. --s 200 --q 2 --v 5.2	
OBJ54	Festive Mailbox v.2	Watercolor scene of children excitedly checking a festive mailbox, eager for holiday greetings. Plain background. Emphasis on anticipation and childhood delight. --s 200 --q 2 --v 5.2	
OBJ55	Ribbon & Bows v.1	Watercolor depiction of elegant ribbons and bows, in shades of red and gold, epitomizing festive gift-giving. Isolated white background. Satiny finish on the ribbons. Format: gift's grace. --s 200 --q 2 --v 5.2	
OBJ56	Ribbon & Bows v.2	Watercolor scene of hands gracefully tying a bow with a lush ribbon on a gift. Light background. Emphasis on the art of gift wrapping. Format: gesture of love. --s 200 --q 2 --v 5.2	

Objects

ID	NAME	PROMPT	SAMPLE RESULT
OBJ57	Eggnog Mug v.1	Watercolor representation of a creamy mug of eggnog, topped with a sprinkle of nutmeg, signaling holiday warmth. Isolated white background. Creamy texture emphasized. Format: sip of tradition. --s 200 --q 2 --v 5.2	
OBJ58	Eggnog Mug v.2	Watercolor scene of hands wrapping around a steaming mug of eggnog, with cookies on the side. Plain background. Focus on the comforting embrace of the drink. Format: festive comfort. --s 200 --q 2 --v 5.2	
OBJ59	Snow-Covered Lantern Post v.1	Watercolor illustration of an old-fashioned lantern post, covered in a soft layer of snow, casting a warm glow. Isolated white background. Format: beacon of warmth. --s 200 -- q 2 --v 5.2	
OBJ60	Snow-Covered Lantern Post v.2	Watercolor scene of a snowy pathway, illuminated by multiple snow-covered lantern posts, leading to a festive home. Light background. Mood of welcoming and coziness captured. --s 200 --q 2 --v 5.2	
OBJ61	Festive Rug v.1	Watercolor rendering of a festive rug, with intricate patterns of holly, bells, and snowflakes. Isolated white background. Fine detailing on the weave and patterns. Format: underfoot festivity. --s 200 --q 2 --v 5.2	

Festive Feasts for the Eyes

Prepare for a visual feast that's as delightful as the season's flavors. Think of golden pies, succulent roasts, and cookies straight from a Christmas storybook, all ready to stir up your festive spirit.

Food

ID	NAME	PROMPT	SAMPLE RESULT
FD01	German Bread v.1	Watercolor depiction of freshly baked German fruit bread wrapped in a festive red and green cloth, placed on a wooden cutting board against an isolated, plain background. Format: high detail. --s 200 --q 2 --v 5.2	
FD02	German Bread v.2	Watercolor portrayal of a rustic German fruit bread loaf with an olive branch on top against an isolated light background. Soft brushwork for a warm feel. Format: portrait. --s 200 --q 2 --v 5.2	
FD03	Christmas Teatime v.1	Watercolor scene of a classic teapot pouring steaming tea into a cup, surrounded by Christmas cookies and sprigs of holly on a white background. Delicate shading for a cozy atmosphere. --s 200 --q 2 --v 5.2	
FD04	Christmas Teatime v.2	Watercolor representation of a festive teacup filled with hot tea, steam rising, with a cinnamon stick and star anise floating on top against a plain background. Detailed brushwork on the steam. --s 200 --q 2 --v 5.2	
FD05	Mulled Wine v.1	Watercolor visual of a glass mug filled with steaming mulled wine, adorned with a cinnamon stick and orange slices against a light background. Vibrant coloring for a warm sensation. --s 200 --q 2 --v 5.2	
FD06	Mulled Wine v.2	Watercolor artwork of a pot of mulled wine on a stove, surrounded by ingredients: star anise, cloves, and citrus slices on a white background. Emphasis on the warm, inviting glow. Format: still life. --s 200 --q 2 --v 5.2	
FD07	Yule Log Cake v.1	Watercolor presentation of a yule log cake decorated with holly and powdered sugar, resembling a snow-covered log, against a plain background. Rich colors with smooth shading. --s 200 --q 2 --v 5.2	

Food

ID	NAME	PROMPT	SAMPLE RESULT
FD08	Yule Log Cake v.2	Watercolor display of a slice of yule log cake revealing its creamy center, placed on a festive plate with a fork, against a light background. Detailed brushwork for a delicious look. Format: close-up. --s 200 --q 2 --v 5.2	
FD09	Roasted Turkey v.1	Watercolor scene of a golden-brown roasted turkey on a platter, garnished with rosemary and cranberries, ready for a Christmas feast against a white background. Soft, warm shading for an appetizing feel. --s 200 --q 2 --v 5.2	
FD10	Roasted Turkey v.2	Watercolor portrayal of a carving knife and fork slicing into a roasted turkey, steam escaping, against a plain background. Emphasis on the juicy texture. Format: action shot. --s 200 --q 2 --v 5.2	
FD11	Christmas Pudding v.1	Watercolor depiction of a steaming Christmas pudding adorned with a sprig of holly and set aflame, against a white background. Lively coloring for a traditional feel. Format: round detail. --s 200 --q 2 --v 5.2	
FD12	Christmas Pudding v.2	Watercolor presentation of a slice of Christmas pudding with a dollop of brandy butter melting atop, placed on a decorative plate against a plain background. Emphasis on the rich textures. --s 200 --q 2 --v 5.2	
FD13	Eggnog Delight v.1	Watercolor visual of a crystal glass filled with creamy eggnog, topped with whipped cream and a sprinkle of nutmeg, against a white background. Smooth blending for a creamy look. --s 200 --q 2 --v 5.2	
FD14	Eggnog Delight v.2	Watercolor representation of a pitcher of eggnog surrounded by ingredients: eggs, nutmeg, and cinnamon sticks, set against a plain background. Emphasis on the rich, inviting hues. --s 200 --q 2 --v 5.2	

Food

ID	NAME	PROMPT	SAMPLE RESULT
FD15	Mince Pies v.1	Watercolor artwork of a single mince pie with a star-shaped pastry top, placed next to a glass of milk, set against a plain background. Detailed brushwork for a festive look. Format: snack time. --s 200 --q 2 --v 5.2	
FD16	Mince Pies v.2	Watercolor scene of a plate of mince pies dusted with powdered sugar, one pie cut open revealing its fruity filling, against a light background. Rich colors. Format: platter view. --s 200 --q 2 --v 5.2	
FD17	Fruitcake v.1	Watercolor display of a rich, dense fruitcake topped with glazed fruits and nuts, sliced open, against a white background. Emphasis on the colorful ingredients. Format: festive centerpiece. --s 200 --q 2 --v 5.2	
FD18	Fruitcake v.2	Watercolor depiction of a slice of fruitcake on a gold-rimmed plate, with a fork, against a plain background. Soft shading capturing the moist texture. Format: dessert detail. --s 200 --q 2 --v 5.2	
FD19	Candy Bowl	Watercolor portrayal of a crystal bowl filled with colorful Christmas candies, with a few spilled around, set against a light background. Vivid coloring for a festive vibe. Format: table centerpiece. --s 200 --q 2 --v 5.2	
FD20	Peppermint Stick	Watercolor artwork of peppermint sticks placed in a mug of hot cocoa, melting and infusing flavor, against a plain background. Soft blending for a cozy look. Format: drink detail. --s 200 --q 2 --v 5.2	
FD21	Roasted Almonds	Watercolor visualization of warm roasted almonds spread on a wooden board, sprinkled with sea salt, against a white background. Detailed shading to capture the roasted texture. --s 200 --q 2 --v 5.2	

Food

ID	NAME	PROMPT	SAMPLE RESULT
FD22	Cranberry Sauce v.1	Watercolor scene of a crystal bowl brimming with glistening cranberry sauce, a silver spoon resting alongside, set against a light background. Lustrous coloring for a festive touch. --s 200 --q 2 --v 5.2	
FD23	Cranberry Sauce v.2	Watercolor depiction of cranberries being cooked in a pot, transforming into a thick sauce, against a plain background. Detailed brushwork. Format: preparation process. --s 200 --q 2 --v 5.2	
FD24	Warm Cinnamon Buns v.1	Watercolor artwork of freshly baked cinnamon buns, steam rising, drizzled with vanilla glaze, set against a white background. Soft blending to capture the warmth and aroma. Format: breakfast scene. --s 200 --q 2 --v 5.2	
FD25	Warm Cinnamon Buns v.2	Watercolor representation of a close-up of a cinnamon bun, revealing its swirled layers and filling, placed on a rustic plate, against a plain background. Format: dessert close-up. --s 200 --q 2 --v 5.2	

Christmas Characters Galore

Greet the beloved icons of the season: the merry Santa Claus, energetic elves, gracious snow queens, and wide-eyed children captivated by the holiday magic.

Characters

ID	NAME	PROMPT	SAMPLE RESULT
CH01	Santa Claus v.1	Watercolor depiction of Santa Claus, jovially laughing with a sack of toys over his shoulder, set against an isolated background. Fine brushwork for the details of his attire. Format: festive icon. --s 200 --q 2 --v 5.2	
CH02	Santa Claus v.2	Watercolor image of Santa reviewing his list in his workshop, surrounded by packed gifts, with a light background. Detailed shading. Format: calm before the storm. --s 200 --q 2 --v 5.2	
CH03	Ice Queen v.1	Watercolor depiction of the Ice Queen in a sparkling gown, her crown glistening, holding a frosty scepter, isolated on a white background. Emphasis on majestic coldness. --s 200 --q 2 --v 5.2	
CH04	Ice Queen v.2	Watercolor scene of the Ice Queen in her icy palace, frost patterns adorning the walls, set against a light background. Delicate shading to capture the shimmer. Format: palace of frost. --s 200 --q 2 --v 5.2	
CH05	Festive Snow Queen v.1	Watercolor portrayal of the Snow Queen in a festive gown, snowflakes swirling around her, isolated on a white background. Emphasis on holiday magic. Format: enchantress of snow. --s 200 --q 2 --v 5.2	
CH06	Festive Snow Queen v.2	Watercolor art of the Snow Queen amidst a winter forest, animals gathered in reverence, set against a light background. Soft brushwork for a whimsical touch. Format: woodland celebration. --s 200 --q 2 --v 5.2	
CH07	Santa's Helpers Wrapping Gifts v.1	Watercolor visualization of Santa's helpers, bustling around, wrapping gifts with bows and ribbons, isolated on a white background. Emphasis on festive industriousness. --s 200 --q 2 --v 5.2	

Characters

ID	NAME	PROMPT	SAMPLE RESULT
CH08	Santa's Helpers Wrapping Gifts v.2	Watercolor depiction of elves collaborating, wrapping toys and stacking them in Santa's sleigh, set against a light background. Detailed shading for a sense of depth. Format: preparing the sleigh. --s 200 --q 2 --v 5.2	
CH09	Nutcracker Ballerina v.1	Watercolor art of the Nutcracker Ballerina, poised gracefully, her tutu adorned with snowflakes, isolated on a white background. Emphasis on festive elegance. Format: dance of the snowflakes. --s 200 --q 2 --v 5.2	
CH10	Nutcracker Ballerina v.2	Watercolor scene of the Ballerina performing on a grand stage, Nutcracker soldiers in the backdrop, set against a light background. Soft brushwork for a dreamlike ambiance. --s 200 --q 2 --v 5.2	
CH11	Kid Christmas Eve Scene v.1	Watercolor illustration of a child, clad in pajamas, trying to sneak a peek at Santa, isolated on a white background. Emphasis on innocent curiosity. Format: quiet anticipation. --s 200 --q 2 --v 5.2	
CH12	Kid Christmas Eve Scene v.2	Watercolor portrayal of a cozy room, a child gazing out of the window at the snowy night, milk and cookies set for Santa, set against a light background. Delicate shading for warmth. --s 200 --q 2 --v 5.2	
CH13	Children Opening Gifts v.1	Watercolor art of joyful children, eyes wide with excitement, unwrapping vibrant Christmas gifts, isolated on a white background. Emphasis on pure elation. Format: morning delight. --s 200 --q 2 --v 5.2	
CH14	Children Opening Gifts v.2	Watercolor visualization of a cozy living room, children eagerly tearing open presents beneath a decorated tree, set against a light background. Soft shading for warmth. Format: festive frenzy. --s 200 --q 2 --v 5.2	

Characters

ID	NAME	PROMPT	SAMPLE RESULT
CH15	Carol Singers v.1	Watercolor representation of a group of carol singers, clad in winter coats and scarves, holding songbooks, isolated on a white background. Emphasis on harmonic unity. Format: voices of joy. --s 200 --q 2 --v 5.2	
CH16	Carol Singers v.2	Watercolor painting of carolers singing outside snow-covered houses, lanterns illuminating their faces, set against a light background. Detailed brushwork. Format: melodies in the snow. --s 200 --q 2 --v 5.2	
CH17	Elderly Couple Exchange Gifts v.1	Watercolor portrayal of an elderly couple, seated by the fireplace, surprise evident on their faces as they unwrap gifts, set against a white background. Format: heartwarming scene. --s 200 --q 2 --v 5.2	
CH18	Elderly Couple Exchange Gifts v.2	Watercolor scene of an elderly couple, exchanging wrapped presents, with twinkling Christmas lights around them, set against a light background. Format: festive moments. --s 200 --q 2 --v 5.2	
CH19	Holy Angels v.1	Watercolor art of multiple holy angels, singing carols in celestial harmony, their robes glowing in soft light, set against a plain background. Intense shading for depth. White background. --s 200 --q 2 --v 5.2	
CH20	Holy Angels v.2	Watercolor representation of a holy angel, gracefully descending with golden halo and wings, amidst floating clouds, set against an isolated background. Format: divine messenger. --s 200 --q 2 --v 5.2	
CH21	Children Choir v.1	Watercolor scene of a children's choir, all dressed in festive white robes with red scarves, holding songbooks and singing carols. Isolated white background. Light brush strokes. Format: festive mood. --s 200 --q 2 --v 5.2	

Characters

ID	NAME	PROMPT	SAMPLE RESULT
CH22	Children Choir v.2	Watercolor portrayal of a children's choir, with each member in green and red festive attire, standing under twinkling Christmas lights. Use varied brush strokes to show the movement of the children. --s 200 --q 2 --v 5.2	
CH23	Festive Elf	Watercolor illustration of a festive elf, adorned in a green suit with red trims, curiously peeking from behind a gift box. Isolated white background. Format: Santa's little helper. --s 200 --q 2 --v 5.2	
CH24	Wise Men	Watercolor portrayal of the three Wise Men in regal attire, each carrying their symbolic gift, isolated on a white background. Emphasis on reverence and grandeur. Format: journey of faith. --s 200 --q 2 --v 5.2	
CH25	Shepherds	Watercolor illustration of shepherds with their flock, an angel appearing above, sharing good tidings, isolated on a white background. Emphasis on rustic humility. Format: heralded news. --s 200 --q 2 --v 5.2	

Action-Packed Holiday Scenes

Leap into lively scenes: from joyous carolers spreading cheer, to exhilarating sleigh rides under the stars, and the bustling excitement of eleventh-hour gift hunting.

Action scenes

ID	NAME	PROMPT	SAMPLE RESULT
AS01	Children Making Snowman v.1	Watercolor depiction of children bundled up in winter attire, laughing as they roll large snowballs and place a carrot for the snowman's nose. Isolated white background. Format: winter fun. --s 200 --q 2 --v 5.2	
AS02	Children Making Snowman v.2	Watercolor scene of kids placing a top hat on their freshly made snowman, with scarves fluttering in the chilly breeze. Light background showing snow- covered trees. Format: festive creation. --s 200 --q 2 --v 5.2	
AS03	Children Sliding v.1	Watercolor of joyful children sliding down a snow-covered hill on sleds, their faces flushed with excitement. Isolated white background. Fluid brushwork. Format: winter thrill. --s 200 --q 2 --v 5.2	
AS04	Children Sliding v.2	Watercolor illustration of kids giggling as they slide down a snowy slope, holding hands in a chain. Plain background. Capture the shimmer of snow using dotted brush techniques. --s 200 --q 2 --v 5.2	
AS05	Secret Santa Gift Exchange v.1	Watercolor portrayal of friends gathered around a festively decorated tree, eagerly exchanging wrapped gifts. Isolated white background. Focus on the intricate patterns of the wrapping paper. --s 200 --q 2 --v 5.2	
AS06	Secret Santa Gift Exchange v.2	Watercolor scene of colleagues laughing and sharing secret Santa gifts, with twinkling fairy lights in the background. Light background. Use varied brush strokes. Format: office holiday. --s 200 --q 2 --v 5.2	
AS07	Children Sneaking Peeks v.1	Watercolor illustration of kids on tiptoes, trying to get a glimpse of Santa placing gifts under the tree. Plain background. Emphasize Santa's silhouette using contrasting colors. --s 200 --q 2 --v 5.2	

Action scenes

ID	NAME	PROMPT	SAMPLE RESULT
AS08	Children Sneaking Peeks v.2	Watercolor depiction of curious children sneaking peeks at their wrapped presents under the tree, their faces illuminated by tree lights. Isolated white background. Delicate shading. --s 200 --q 2 --v 5.2	
AS09	Family Around Fireplace v.1	Watercolor rendering of a family snuggled together, sharing stories by the fireplace with stockings hung nearby. The fire's glow casting a warm light. Subtle shading. Format: cozy evening. --s 200 --q 2 --v 5.2	
AS10	Family Around Fireplace v.2	Watercolor scene of parents and children sipping hot cocoa by the fireplace, the room bathed in the gentle light of the fire. Light background. Soft brushwork. Format: winter warmth. --s 200 --q 2 --v 5.2	
AS11	Mom Baking with Child v.1	Watercolor scene of a mother and child in a warm kitchen, rolling out dough and cutting festive cookie shapes. Flour dusting the air. Isolated white background. Detailed brushwork. --s 200 --q 2 --v 5.2	
AS12	Mom Baking with Child v.2	Watercolor portrayal of a child excitedly decorating cookies while the mother watches with pride. Light background showing a cozy kitchen scene. Format: festive prep. --s 200 --q 2 --v 5.2	
AS13	Christmas Market Couple Walking v.1	Watercolor of a couple strolling hand in hand through a bustling Christmas market, surrounded by stalls selling festive wares and lights twinkling above. Isolated white background. Format: romantic stroll. --s 200 --q 2 --v 5.2	
AS14	Christmas Market Couple Walking v.2	Watercolor depiction of a couple, wrapped up in scarves, exploring a snowy Christmas market with mugs of hot mulled wine. Plain background. Emphasize the steam rising from the mugs. --s 200 --q 2 --v 5.2	

Action scenes

ID	NAME	PROMPT	SAMPLE RESULT
AS15	Santa Feeding Deer v.1	Watercolor portrayal of Santa Claus tenderly feeding his reindeer, with a snowy North Pole landscape behind. Isolated white background. Detailed brushwork on the reindeer's fur. Format: festive care. --s 200 --q 2 --v 5.2	
AS16	Santa Feeding Deer v.2	Watercolor scene of Santa and a young reindeer sharing a moment, with the deer nibbling on some greens from Santa's hand. Light background. Soft strokes to emphasize the ethereal lights. --s 200 --q 2 --v 5.2	
AS17	Santa and Mrs Santa Dancing v.1	Watercolor depiction of Santa and Mrs. Claus sharing a dance, lost in a moment of festive joy. Their laughter echoing, as snow gently falls around. Isolated white background. Format: yuletide waltz. --s 200 --q 2 --v 5.2	
AS18	Santa and Mrs Santa Dancing v.2	Watercolor illustration of Santa and Mrs. Claus dancing under a mistletoe, with elves playing festive tunes in the background. Plain background. Emphasis on the vibrant colors of the scene. --s 200 --q 2 --v 5.2	
AS19	Santa with a Child on his Knee v.1	Watercolor rendering of Santa sitting in his grand chair, a child on his knee whispering their Christmas wish into his ear. Isolated white background. Detailed brushwork on Santa's beard. --s 200 --q 2 --v 5.2	
AS20	Santa with a Child on his Knee v.2	Watercolor scene of a festive grotto where Santa listens intently, his eyes twinkling, to a child sharing their dreams. Light background with shimmering festive lights. Format: magical moment. --s 200 --q 2 --v 5.2	
AS21	Santa Reading the Letters v.1	Watercolor illustration of Santa at his desk, engrossed in reading letters from children all over the world. Isolated white background. Emphasize the variety of handwriting and stamps. --s 200 --q 2 --v 5.2	

Action scenes

ID	NAME	PROMPT	SAMPLE RESULT
AS22	Santa Reading the Letters v.2	Watercolor depiction of Santa and Mrs. Claus sitting by the fireplace, reading children's letters, smiles and occasionally chuckles accompanying. Light background. Format: yuletide duties. --s 200 --q 2 --v 5.2	
AS23	Santa Reading a Book to Children v.1	Watercolor scene of Santa sitting in a cozy corner, a group of enchanted children surrounding him as he narrates a festive tale. Isolated white background. Detailed strokes, book illustrations. --s 200 --q 2 --v 5.2	
AS24	Santa Reading a Book to Children v.2	Watercolor depiction of Santa with children gathered around, captivated by a Christmas story. Light background. Emphasize the eager expressions on the kid's faces. Format: evening tales. --s 200 --q 2 --v 5.2	
AS25	Christmas Caroling v.1	Watercolor illustration of a group of carolers, their faces bright with joy, as they sing festive songs in the snow-clad streets. Isolated white background. Soft brushwork for the winter ambiance. --s 200 --q 2 --v 5.2	
AS26	Christmas Caroling v.2	Watercolor scene of carol singers, each holding a lantern, their voices harmonizing perfectly under the twinkling stars. Light background on snow-covered rooftops. Format: starlit serenade. --s 200 --q 2 --v 5.2	
AS27	Building Gingerbread Houses v.1	Watercolor portrayal of a family around a table, constructing intricate gingerbread houses. Excitement evident candies and frosting together. White backdrop. Format: sweet architecture. --s 200 --q 2 --v 5.2	
AS28	Building Gingerbread Houses v.2	Watercolor scene of children, as they compete to make the best gingerbread house. Behind them, a warm kitchen with holiday preparations. Plain background. Format: festive competition. --s 200 --q 2 --v 5.2	

Action scenes

ID	NAME	PROMPT	SAMPLE RESULT
AS29	Family Decorating the Tree v.1	Watercolor illustration of a family sharing a moment, working together to decorate a tall Christmas tree. The child placing the star atop. Isolated white background. Format: tree traditions. --s 200 --q 2 --v 5.2	
AS30	Family Decorating the Tree v.2	Watercolor depiction of parents lifting their child, helping them hang an ornament on the tree. Light background, with wrapped gifts beneath the tree. Fluid strokes for the tinsel and ribbons. --s 200 --q 2 --v 5.2	
AS31	Kids Hanging Stockings v.1	Watercolor scene of two children on tiptoes, reaching up to hang their stockings on the mantel, eager anticipation in their eyes. Gentle brushwork. Format: festive anticipation. --s 200 --q 2 --v 5.2	
AS32	Kids Hanging Stockings v.2	Watercolor portrayal of siblings, their stockings in hand, excitedly discussing what Santa might bring. A cozy living room setting behind them. Light background. Emphasize the warm atmosphere. --s 200 --q 2 --v 5.2	
AS33	Couple Under the Mistletoe v.1	Watercolor illustration of a couple sharing a tender moment under a hanging mistletoe, their surroundings blurred with festive cheer. Isolated white background. Format: mistletoe magic.--s 200 --q 2 --v 5.2	
AS34	Couple Under the Mistletoe v.2	Watercolor scene of a couple, drawn to each other under a doorway adorned with mistletoe, a mix of surprise and happiness on faces. Plain background. Format: unexpected romance. --s 200 --q 2 --v 5.2	
AS35	Ice Skating on a Pond	Watercolor portrayal of a couple holding hands, ice skating in synchrony, their joy evident. Snowflakes gently falling around them. Light background. Fluid strokes for the flowing movements. --s 200 --q 2 --v 5.2	

Action scenes

ID	NAME	PROMPT	SAMPLE RESULT
AS36	Hot Cocoa by the Fireplace v.1	Watercolor scene of a person wrapped in a blanket, sipping hot cocoa by a roaring fireplace. Isolated white background. Detailed brushwork for the cocoa's steam and marshmallows. Format: comfort. --s 200 --q 2 --v 5.2	
AS37	Hot Cocoa by the Fireplace v.2	Watercolor illustration of a family, mugs of cocoa in hand, exchanging stories beside the fireplace, the room illuminated by the fire's soft glow. Gentle strokes to depict the rich chocolate texture. --s 200 --q 2 --v 5.2	
AS38	Christmas Shopping Rush v.1	Watercolor portrayal of bustling shoppers, their arms laden with colorful Christmas gifts, the winter streets adorned with festive lights. Isolated white background. Detailed rendering. Format: holiday. --s 200 --q 2 --v 5.2	
AS39	Christmas Shopping Rush v.2	Watercolor scene of a snowy street, shoppers hurrying about, storefronts adorned with decorations beckoning them. Light background. Emphasize the snow-capped rooftops and shoppers' trails. --s 200 --q 2 --v 5.2	

Inside a Christmas Haven

Step into the heart of the holiday home, where soft lights twinkle, stockings hang in anticipation, and Christmas trees glisten, inviting you to bask in the cozy glow of the season.

Interiors

ID	NAME	PROMPT	SAMPLE RESULT
IN01	Festive Fireplace v.1	A fireplace scene where a cat snoozes by the warmth, surrounded by wrapped gifts against white background. Use watercolor to capture the cozy and serene mood. --s 200 --q 2 --v 5.2	
IN02	Festive Fireplace v.2	A watercolor depiction of a playful fox with Christmas lights tangled around its tail against a snowy backdrop. Gentle shading and a joyful tone. --s 200 --q 2 --v 5.2	
IN03	Toy Filled Children's Room v.1	Watercolor painting of a children's room overflowing with toys, a train set circling a Christmas tree. Emphasize joy and wonder. Isolated, white background. --s 200 --q 2 --v 5.2	
IN04	Toy Filled Children's Room v.2	A room scene where children in pajamas excitedly play with new Christmas toys. Watercolor. Capture the essence of Christmas morning magic. --s 200 --q 2 --v 5.2	
IN05	Cozy library v.1	Watercolor scene of a cozy library with Christmas festive decorations, where an individual reads by the fireplace. Capture the ambiance of peace and knowledge. Isolated plain background. --s 200 --q 2 --v 5.2	
IN06	Cozy library v.2	A library with snow gently falling outside its window, shelves filled with books, and a Christmas tree in a corner. Emphasize the sanctuary-like feel. --s 200 --q 2 --v 5.2	
IN07	Nostalgic Bedroom v.1	Watercolor bedroom scene decorated with Christmas lights with a frosted window pane, showing outside in the snow, isolated white background. Capture the warmth inside and the joy outside. --s 200 --q 2 --v 5.2	

ID	NAME	PROMPT	SAMPLE RESULT
IN08	Nostalgic Bedroom v.2	Watercolor portrayal of a nostalgic bedroom with vintage Christmas ornaments and an old quilt. Emphasize the memories and the passing of time. Plain background. --s 200 --q 2 --v 5.2	
IN09	Country Style Kitchen v.1	Watercolor kitchen scene with a family preparing Christmas dinner, surrounded by rustic decor. Capture the hustle, bustle, and love. White background. --s 200 --q 2 --v 5.2	
IN10	Country Style Kitchen v.2	A watercolor depiction of a winter country style kitchen, with a pie cooling on the window sill and festive decorations everywhere. Emphasize homey and welcoming vibes. Light background. --s 200 --q 2 --v 5.2	
IN11	Classic Dining Room v.1	Watercolor dining room with a grand chandelier, reflecting on a table laden with festive treats against isolated white background. Highlight the opulence and festive spirit. --s 200 --q 2 --v 5.2	
IN12	Classic Dining Room v.2	A watercolor painting of a classic dining room set for Christmas dinner, with candles, holly, and twinkling lights. Emphasize elegance and tradition. Isolated. Plain background. --s 200 --q 2 --v 5.2	
IN13	Cozy Living Room v.1	Watercolor of a cozy living room, with a family singing carols around a grand piano against white backdrop. Capture the unity and Chrismast festive joy. --s 200 --q 2 --v 5.2	
IN14	Cozy Living Room v.2	A watercolor living room scene where children open their gifts beneath a towering Christmas tree. Emphasize the magic and anticipation. Light background. --s 200 --q 2 --v 5.2	

Interiors

ID	NAME	PROMPT	SAMPLE RESULT
IN15	Gifts in a Snowy Window v.1	Watercolor clipart of wrapped gifts piled high on a windowsill, with snowflakes gently falling outside, against white background. Capture the warmth of giving against the cold. --s 200 --q 2 --v 5.2	
IN16	Gifts in a Snowy Window v.2	A snowy window where each gift's shadow tells a different festive story. Emphasize the mystery and joy of the season. Watercolor. Plain background. --s 200 --q 2 --v 5.2	
IN17	Wintry Balcony View v.1	A balcony scene with a table set for two, surrounded by Christmas decorations and snow. Emphasize the intimate and festive mood. --s 200 --q 2 --v 5.2	
IN18	Wintry Balcony View v.2	Watercolor depiction of a balcony overlooking a snowy cityscape, adorned with festive lights. Capture the serenity and beauty of winter nights. --s 200 --q 2 --v 5.2	
IN19	Elegant Ballroom v.1	A watercolor depiction of an elegant ballroom, with couples dancing beneath a mistletoe against white isolated backdrop. Emphasize the grandeur and festive romance. --s 200 --q 2 --v 5.2	
IN20	Elegant Ballroom v.2	Ballroom scene with a grand Christmas tree, around which children play. Watercolor. Capture the opulence and childlike wonder. Plain background. --s 200 --q 2 -- v 5.2	
IN21	Festive Hallway	Hallway with festive wreaths on each door, and children sneaking around with gifts. Watercolor. Capture the mischief and anticipation. White background. --s 200 --q 2 --v 5.2	

Yuletide in the City

Stroll through the winter-kissed streets, where shop windows sparkle with festive flair and town squares showcase majestic Christmas trees, bringing urban landscapes to festive life.

City / Town

ID	NAME	PROMPT	SAMPLE RESULT
CT01	European Christmas Market v.1	Watercolor representation of a bustling European Christmas market, adorned with twinkling lights and festive stalls, isolated on a white background. Format: panoramic view. --s 200 --q 2 --v 5.2	
CT02	European Christmas Market v.2	Watercolor scene of shoppers enjoying the European Christmas market, with the aroma of mulled wine and festive treats filling the air, against a light background. Format: busy street view. --s 200 --q 2 --v 5.2	
CT03	Village Street View v.1	Watercolor clipart of a quaint village street, snow-covered rooftops and children playing, isolated against a white background. Soft shades for a serene winter morning. Format: early morning. --s 200 --q 2 --v 5.2	
CT04	Village Street View v.2	Watercolor portrayal of villagers preparing for Christmas, decorating homes and setting up trees, with a light background. Brushwork capturing the festive preparations. Format: evening dusk. --s 200 --q 2 --v 5.2	
CT05	Church	Watercolor artwork of a majestic church, its spire reaching to the sky, surrounded by a blanket of snow, isolated on a white background. Format: historical architecture. --s 200 --q 2 --v 5.2	
CT06	Cottage House	Watercolor illustration of a cozy Christmas decorated cottage, isolated against a white background. Detailed shading to capture the rustic charm. Format: countryside retreat. --s 200 --q 2 --v 5.2	
CT07	Bridge Through the River	Watercolor Christmas scene depicting lovers walking hand-in-hand over the bridge with festive lights, set against a light background. Delicate brushwork capturing their shared warmth. --s 200 --q 2 --v 5.2	

City / Town

ID	NAME	PROMPT	SAMPLE RESULT
CT08	Clock Tower v.1	Watercolor portrayal of an ancient clock tower, its hands nearing midnight, signaling Christmas, isolated on a white background. Soft blending impending festive moment. Format: ticking time. --s 200 --q 2 --v 5.2	
CT09	Clock Tower v.2	Watercolor art of townsfolk gathering around a clock tower, waiting for the chime that signals Christmas, set against a light background. Lively brushwork. Format: town square. --s 200 --q 2 --v 5.2	
CT10	Rural Christmas Farm v.1	Watercolor clipart portrayal of a serene rural farm blanketed in snow, with farm animals gathered in the barn, isolated on a white background. Emphasis on simplicity. Format: country peace. --s 200 --q 2 --v 5.2	
CT11	Rural Christmas Farm v.2	Watercolor depiction of farmers setting up a Christmas tree outside their farmhouse, set against a light background. Lively brushwork capturing their joyous spirits. Format: farming festivity. --s 200 --q 2 --v 5.2	
CT12	Christmas Windmill v.1	Watercolor art of an old windmill, its sails adorned with Christmas festive lights, isolated against a white background. Emphasis on historical charm. Format: windmill wonder. --s 200 --q 2 --v 5.2	
CT13	Christmas Windmill v.2	Watercolor scene of children playing near a windmill, sledging down a snow-covered hill, with a light background. Detailed shading capturing their playful energy. Format: winter playtime. --s 200 --q 2 --v 5.2	
CT14	Observatory v.1	Watercolor visualization of an observatory, its dome open to the winter skies, isolated on a white background. Muted colors for a night of stargazing. Format: stars above. --s 200 --q 2 --v 5.2	

City / Town

ID	NAME	PROMPT	SAMPLE RESULT
CT15	Observatory v.2	Watercolor representation of families visiting the observatory to view the Christmas star, set against a light background. Emphasis on wonder and discovery. Format: festive stargazing. --s 200 --q 2 --v 5.2	
CT16	Bakery House v.1	Watercolor painting of a quaint bakery, its windows steamed up from the baking, displaying festive pastries, isolated on a white background. Soft shades for a warm interior. Format: Christmas treats. --s 200 -- q 2 --v 5.2	
CT17	Bakery House v.2	Watercolor portrayal of villagers buying Christmas goodies from the bakery, the aroma of cinnamon in the air, set against a light background. Lively brushwork. Format: festive shopping. --s 200 --q 2 --v 5.2	
CT18	Toy Store v.1	Watercolor illustration of an old-fashioned toy store, its windows adorned with festive decorations and filled with wooden toys, isolated on a white background. Format: vintage festivity. --s 200 --q 2 --v 5.2	
CT19	Toy Store v.2	Watercolor scene of children with rosy cheeks pressed against the glass of a toy store, set against a light background. Detailed shading to emphasize their anticipation. Format: Christmas wish. --s 200 --q 2 --v 5.2	
CT20	Decorated Christmas Mansion v.1	Watercolor art of a grand mansion lavishly decorated for Christmas, its gates open to welcome guests, isolated on a white background. Emphasis on opulence. Format: regal celebration. --s 200 --q 2 --v 5.2	
CT21	Decorated Christmas Mansion v.2	Watercolor scene of carolers singing outside a mansion, their breath visible in the cold, set against a light background. Detailed shading for depth. Format: melodies of the season. --s 200 --q 2 --v 5.2	

City / Town

ID	NAME	PROMPT	SAMPLE RESULT
CT22	Ice Skating Rink v.1	Watercolor representation of families visiting the observatory to view the Christmas star, set against a light background. Emphasis on wonder and discovery. Format: festive stargazing. --s 200 --q 2 --v 5.2	
CT23	Ice Skating Rink v.2	Watercolor painting of an ice skating rink in the town square, surrounded by twinkling fairy lights, isolated on a white background. Emphasis on winter fun. Format: glide and twirl. --s 200 --q 2 --v 5.2	
CT24	Snow-Covered City Alley v.1	Watercolor clipart of a narrow city alley, its cobblestones hidden under fresh snow, the glow of lanterns creating long shadows, isolated on a white background. Emphasis on quiet winter night. --s 200 --q 2 --v 5.2	
CT25	Snow-Covered City Alley v.2	Watercolor scene of an alley where children sneak around, engaged in a playful snowball fight, set against a light background. Lively brushwork capturing their energy. Format: snowball ambush. --s 200 --q 2 --v 5.2	
CT26	Christmas Boat at the Dock v.1	Watercolor illustration of a wooden boat at the dock, adorned with Christmas lights, isolated on a white background. Emphasis on tranquil waterfront. Format: serene anchorage. --s 200 --q 2 --v 5.2	
CT27	Christmas Boat at the Dock v.2	Watercolor scene of families gathered on the boat, singing carols and sharing gifts, set against a light background. Detailed shading to reflect the festive mood. Format: harbor celebration. --s 200 --q 2 --v 5.2	

Nature's Winter Cloak

Behold the serene beauty of Christmas in the great outdoors: majestic mountains dusted with snow, icy lakes glistening under the moonlight, and forests that whisper tales of winter's enchantment.

Nature

ID	NAME	PROMPT	SAMPLE RESULT
NT01	Winter Forest v.1	Watercolor depiction of a silent winter festive forest, where snow-covered pines stand tall against a white background. Emphasize the serenity and untouched beauty. --s 200 --q 2 --v 5.2	
NT02	Winter Forest v.2	Watercolor forest scene with animals quietly moving through, leaving tracks in the fresh snow. Capture the life within the stillness. White background. --s 200 --q 2 --v 5.2	
NT03	Small House in the Mountains v.1	Watercolor portrayal of a secluded mountain house, smoke rising from its chimney against the snowy backdrop. Capture the isolation and coziness. --s 200 -- q 2 --v 5.2	
NT04	Small House in the Mountains v.2	Watercolor a snow-covered house with lights gleaming warmly from its windows, nestled between towering alpine peaks. Emphasize contrast and comfort. White background. --s 200 --q 2 --v 5.2	
NT05	Santa's North Pole v.1	Watercolor painting of Santa's North Pole workshop, bustling with elves preparing gifts. Capture the energy and magic of the scene. White background. --s 200 --q 2 --v 5.2	
NT06	Santa's North Pole v.2	Watercolor serene North Pole scene where Santa reads a long list with a reindeer peeking over. Emphasize the anticipation and warmth. White background. --s 200 --q 2 --v 5.2	
NT07	Northern Lights Landscape v.1	Watercolor landscape where the Northern Lights playfully illuminate a snow-covered forest. Capture the surreal and mesmerizing beauty. Isolated white background. --s 200 --q 2 --v 5.2	

Nature

ID	NAME	PROMPT	SAMPLE RESULT
NT08	Northern Lights Landscape v.2	Watercolor depiction of the Northern Lights dancing vividly across a starry sky, reflecting on a frozen lake below. Emphasize the wonder and natural magic. --s 200 --q 2 --v 5.2	
NT09	Festive Mountain Resort v.1	Whatercolor a mountain resort where families gather around bonfires, singing carols under the starry sky against isolated white background. Emphasize the community and celebration. --s 200 --q 2 --v 5.2	
NT10	Festive Mountain Resort v.2	Watercolor scene of a festive mountain resort, with skiers by day and a grand Christmas tree by night. Capture the thrill and festive spirit. --s 200 -- q 2 --v 5.2	
NT11	Alpine Snowfall v.1	Whatercolor alpine scene with towering peaks under a gentle snowfall, creating a blanket of white. Emphasize the majesty and tranquility. White background. --s 200 --q 2 --v 5.2	
NT12	Alpine Snowfall v.2	Watercolor painting of an alpine village, rooftops dusted with fresh snowfall, and children playing below. Capture the charm and whimsy. --s 200 --q 2 --v 5.2	
NT13	Winter Pine Tree v.1	Whitercolor a pine tree adorned with natural ornaments like pinecones and birds, under a snowy canopy against white background. Capture the life and beauty in solitude. --s 200 --q 2 --v 5.2	
NT14	Winter Pine Tree v.2	Watercolor depiction of a solitary pine tree, laden with snow, standing resilient against a plain background. Emphasize the simplicity and strength. --s 200 --q 2 --v 5.2	

Nature

ID	NAME	PROMPT	SAMPLE RESULT
NT15	Snowy Meadow	Watercolor clipart painting of a snowy meadow where deer graze peacefully, surrounded by a soft, against white backdrop. Capture the serenity and life. --s 200 --q 2 --v 5.2	
NT16	Frozen Waterfall v.1	Whatercolor a mountain resort where families gather around bonfires, singing carols under the starry sky against isolated white background. Emphasize the community and celebration. --s 200 --q 2 --v 5.2	
NT17	Frozen Waterfall v.2	Watercolor depiction of a frozen waterfall, icicles shimmering in the winter sun, set against a plain background. Emphasize the stillness and brilliance. --s 200 -- q 2 --v 5.2	
NT18	Ice-covered Pond v.1	Watercolor clipart of serene pond covered with a layer of ice, reflecting the trees and sky above against white plain backdrop. Capture the calm and reflection. --s 200 --q 2 --v 5.2	
NT19	Ice-covered Pond v.2	Watercolor clipart scene of an ice-covered pond where children skate, their breath visible in the cold air against white background. Emphasize the joy and crisp atmosphere. --s 200 --q 2 --v 5.2	
NT20	Christmas Garden v.1	Watercolor depiction of a Christmas garden, with snow-covered topiaries and holly bushes, set against a white plain background. Emphasize the festive greenery and design. --s 200 --q 2 --v 5.2	
NT21	Christmas Garden v.2	Watercolor a garden pathway leading to a gazebo, decorated with lights and wreaths. Capture the invitation and warmth amidst the cold. White background. --s 200 --q 2 --v 5.2	

Outdoor Festivities Unfold

Join in the outdoor holiday jubilation, from the joy of rolling the perfect snowman to the bustling charm of Christmas markets under the open sky.

Outdoor

ID	NAME	PROMPT	SAMPLE RESULT
OTD01	Snowman v.1	Watercolor depiction of a classic snowman with a top hat, carrot nose, and coal eyes, set against a white background. Emphasize the whimsical nature and joy of winter. --s 200 --q 2 --v 5.2	
OTD02	Snowman v.2	Watercolor a scene of children laughing and building a snowman, with winter trees in the backdrop. Capture the happiness of shared moments. White background. --s 200 --q 2 --v 5.2	
OTD03	Christmas Postbox	Watercolor painting of a red Christmas postbox, dusted with snow, awaiting letters to Santa. Emphasize the anticipation and magic of the season. --s 200 --q 2 --v 5.2	
OTD04	Ornate Doors v.1	Watercolor portrayal of ornate doors adorned with festive wreaths and golden knockers, set against a white background. Emphasize the elegance and mystery. --s 200 --q 2 --v 5.2	
OTD05	Ornate Doors v.2	Watercolor doors opening to reveal a cozy interior with a blazing fireplace. Capture the warmth and invitation of home during winter. --s 200 --q 2 --v 5.2	
OTD06	Festive Sleds v.1	Watercolor a sled parked beside a pine tree, awaiting a festive journey, set against a plain background. Capture the anticipation and tradition. --s 200 --q 2 --v 5.2	
OTD07	Festive Sleds v.2	Watercolor depiction of festive sleds laden with gifts, sliding down a snowy hill. Emphasize the thrill and joy of the festive ride. --s 200 --q 2 --v 5.2	

Outdoor

ID	NAME	PROMPT	SAMPLE RESULT
OTD08	Christmas Carousel	Watercolor scene of a Christmas carousel, illuminated with fairy lights, with children laughing and riding. Happy moment. White background. --s 200 --q 2 --v 5.2	
OTD09	Christmas Caravan Camper v.1	Watercolor a camper with children peeking out, a snowman nearby, set against a plain background. Capture the joy of a winter road trip. White background. --s 200 --q 2 --v 5.2	
OTD10	Christmas Caravan Camper v.2	Watercolor painting of a Christmas caravan camper, lit up with festive lights, parked in a snow-covered field. Emphasize the adventure and coziness. --s 200 --q 2 --v 5.2	
OTD11	Campfire v.1	Watercolor a campfire scene where stories are shared under a starry winter sky. Capture the tradition and warmth of shared moments. White background. --s 200 --q 2 --v 5.2	
OTD12	Campfire v.2	Watercolor depiction of a campfire in the snow, with families gathered around, roasting marshmallows. Emphasize the warmth and community. --s 200 --q 2 --v 5.2	
OTD13	Frosted Winter Window v.1	Watercolor a window pane where a child's hand draws festive patterns on the frost. Capture the wonder and creativity of winter. White background. --s 200 --q 2 --v 5.2	
OTD14	Frosted Winter Window v.2	Watercolor portrayal of a frosted winter window, with patterns of ice crystals, set against a white background. Emphasize the beauty and intricacy. --s 200 --q 2 --v 5.2	

Outdoor

ID	NAME	PROMPT	SAMPLE RESULT
OTD15	Winter Gazebo v.1	A gazebo where a couple dances to silent snowfall, capturing the romance and magic of winter. --s 200 --q 2 --v 5.2	
OTD16	Winter Gazebo v.2	Watercolor scene of a winter gazebo adorned with fairy lights, set in a snowy garden. Emphasize the serenity and elegance. --s 200 --q 2 --v 5.2	
OTD17	Christmas Tree Farm v.1	A tree farm blanketed in snow, with a wooden sign pointing to "Santa's Workshop." Capture the wonder and adventure. --s 200 --q 2 --v 5.2	
OTD18	Christmas Tree Farm v.2	Watercolor scene of a Christmas tree farm, families choosing their perfect tree. Emphasize the tradition and joy of the season. --s 200 --q 2 --v 5.2	
OTD19	Snowy Pathways v.1	Watercolor clipart of pathway illuminated by festive lanterns, with children sledging down, set against a plain background. Capture the fun and luminance of winter. White background. --s 200 --q 2 --v 5.2	
OTD20	Snowy Pathways v.2	Watercolor depiction of snowy pathways leading to a distant cottage, footsteps marking the way. Emphasize the journey and destination. --s 200 --q 2 --v 5.2	
OTD21	Moonlit Snowy Night	Watercolor a scene where a lone wolf howls under the moon, capturing the wilderness and enchantment of winter nights. White background. --s 200 --q 2 --v 5.2	

Ornamental Stories

Zoom in on the delicate artistry of Christmas decorations: fragile glass baubles, handcrafted star-toppers, and cherished ornaments that hold the legacy of holidays gone by.

Ornaments

ID	NAME	PROMPT	
ORN01	Star Topper v.1	Watercolor depiction of a shimmering gold star topper, intricately designed with swirls and sparkles, isolated on a white background. Emphasis on festive elegance. Format: pinnacle of the tree. --s 200 --q 2 --v 5.2	
ORN02	Star Topper v.2	Watercolor illustration of a star topper glistening atop a beautifully decorated Christmas tree, set against a light background. Soft brushwork. Format: tree's crowning glory. --s 200 --q 2 --v 5.2	
ORN03	Christmas Tinsel v.1	Watercolor visualization of flowing silver tinsel strands, twinkling as they catch the light, isolated on a white background. Emphasis on radiant shimmer. Format: sparkling festivity. --s 200 --q 2 --v 5.2	
ORN04	Christmas Tinsel v.2	Watercolor portrayal of a Christmas tree adorned with glistening tinsel, set against a light background. Detailed shading to capture the play of light. Format: tinsel's embrace. --s 200 --q 2 --v 5.2	
ORN05	Angel Ornament	Watercolor art of a delicate angel ornament, with wings outstretched and a halo of light, isolated on a white background. Emphasis on celestial beauty. Format: guardian of the festivities. --s 200 --q 2 --v 5.2	
ORN06	Snowflake Ornament	Watercolor painting of a crystal snowflake ornament, each branch intricately detailed, isolated on a white background. Emphasis on winter's artistry. Format: unique crystalline. --s 200 --q 2 --v 5.2	
ORN07	Handmade Clay Ornaments v.1	Watercolor depiction of an assortment of handmade clay ornaments, each with its unique festive design, isolated on a white background. Emphasis on rustic charm. Format: artisanal treasures. --s 200 --q 2 --v 5.2	

NAME		PROMPT	SAMPLE RESULT
ORN08	Handmade Clay Ornaments v.2	Watercolor visualization of a Christmas tree decorated with various handmade clay ornaments, set against a light background. Soft brushwork. Format: crafted with love. --s 200 --q 2 --v 5.2	
ORN09	Retro Toy Soldiers v.1	Watercolor illustration of retro toy soldiers in formation, their uniforms vibrant and polished, isolated on a white background. Emphasis on nostalgic allure. Format: toys on parade. --s 200 --q 2 --v 5.2	
ORN10	Retro Toy Soldiers v.2	Watercolor scene of toy soldiers guarding a mountain of wrapped gifts under a Christmas tree, set against a light background. Lively brushwork capturing their animated stance. Format: guardians of joy. --s 200 --q 2 --v 5.2	
ORN11	Vintage Glass Baubles	Watercolor art of a collection of vintage glass baubles, their surfaces reflecting the lights of the season, isolated on a white background. Emphasis on timeless elegance. Format: yesteryear's glow. --s 200 --q 2 --v 5.2	
ORN12	Holy Leaves	Watercolor depiction of fresh holly leaves, their deep green contrasted with bright red berries, isolated on a white background. Emphasis on festive freshness. Format: nature's ornament. --s 200 --q 2 --v 5.2	

Contacts

A Big Thank You!

You've dived into the pages of this book and swam through the sea of creativity — thank you for bringing your imagination along for the ride! It's creators like you who add vibrant strokes to the canvas of digital art.

Share Your Thoughts

If these prompts have ignited your creative spark, I'd be over the moon to see a 5-star review from you! Your support not only fuels my passion but also guides fellow creators to this collection of digital inspiration.

Got Questions? Let's Chat!

If you hit a creative snag or just want to chat about your journey, don't hesitate to drop a line. We're all about making your experience as smooth and enjoyable as possible.

Email: hello@movetoai.tech

Instagram: https://instagram.com/movetoai/

* 9 7 9 8 8 6 6 4 3 5 1 2 8 *